# THE

# STANISLAVSKI

# METHOD

## KONSTANTIN S. STANISLAVSKI
as Gayev in Chekhov's *The Cherry Orchard*

# THE

# Stanislavski

## METHOD

## The professional training
## of an actor

Digested from the teachings of
Konstantin S. Stanislavski by

# SONIA MOORE

THE VIKING PRESS · NEW YORK

# CONTENTS

## Contents

# PREFACE

## BY Sir John Gielgud

I have never really believed that acting can be taught. Yet, when I remember what a clumsy beginner I was myself and how greatly I have been influenced, all through my long stage career, by the fine directors and players with whom I have been fortunate enough to be associated, I cannot deny the advantage of teaching, provided it can be followed up by hard personal experience. Let nobody imagine, however, that he can learn to act from reading books, however intelligent or profound they may be, about the art of acting.

All creative art can be studied, of course. When one is young, one imitates the players one most admires as artists copy great pictures in the galleries. But, as the theater is an imitation of life, so it is as ephemeral and intangible as life itself (in a way that music, painting, and literature are not), and it changes in every decade and generation. One cannot copy acting, or even what seems to be the method of acting. One has to experiment and discover one's own way of expression for oneself, and one never ceases to be dissatisfied. The quality and development of one's work changes with the degree of responsiveness and sureness of technique which one has acquired over the years. One is affected, too, by the style and quality of the work in hand, the respect or dissatisfaction one may have with one's material, and by one's own personal reactions to directors and fellow players, to the author, to the play itself.

There are so many lessons in the theater to be learned: application, concentration, self-discipline, the use of the voice and the body, imagination, observation, simplification, self-criticism. Often the "tradition" of the theater seems to be at odds with the modern expression of original contemporary acting. I believe that one is as important as the other and that one should study and learn from both. One's basic technical equipment should be perfected in order to enable one to relax, to simplify, to cut away dead wood.

Just as one moves, in real life, from one phase to another, experiencing almost imperceptible developments along the road as one gets older and one's personal and professional experiences lead one to make new discoveries about oneself and life in general, so it is hard to pin down on paper any practical guide to help an individual actor to select the best means of discovering the wellsprings of his art—how he can draw from his own sensitivity the power to command an audience and fascinate them by his interpretation of emotions given him in a particular form by the playwright and presented by him with the guidance of the director. Since he is not the sole creator, but only an instrument working in an uncertain medium (gloriously flexible yet desperately fallible), he needs all the more to have his physical and vocal means under strict control. He must think about his work in the many hours when he is not actually practicing it, about how to cherish his powers of imagination so that he can summon them at will just at the time he needs them. He has to perform before a living audience eight times a week, after achieving a more or less finished performance in the three or four short weeks at his disposal for rehearsal, working perhaps with a director and actors with whom he may not be in sympathy. Even before this he may have had to convince a director, in a few short minutes, that he is competent to play a role for which many others are also being considered.

This book is full of good and useful observations on the study and practice of acting. It says, simply and clearly, many wise things about the art of the theater. Stanislavski's two great books are complicated and sometimes difficult—at any rate for a young actor—to digest in full. Here is an admirable précis of some of his practical wisdom; a still further proof, if one is needed, of the legacy he has left behind to carry on his own example and devotion to the theater which he served so greatly.

# FOREWORD

## BY Joshua Logan

Perhaps Konstantin Stanislavski was a legend before his death in 1938. He is certainly a legend now. All over the world actors, directors, students, and teachers of acting are quoting his writings and following his teachings. Here in America new words have sprung up in theater language. For years the phrase "Stanislavski's method" was used in theatrical conversations. Now it's simply "the method." We hear phrases like "he's a method actor," "method writing," "method directing." All this, I believe, has stimulated interest in the theater and is producing some great results.

How did all of this start? Who put the word "method" into our language? Who was Stanislavski? What did he really believe? What did he really teach?

In the winter of 1930 and 1931 I had the unique opportunity of studying with Stanislavski in his studio home in Moscow and of watching him direct rehearsals. Along with my fellow student, the late Charles Leatherbee, I had tea with the great man and his lovely wife each day after rehearsals. I also met and talked with Nemirovich-Danchenko, the equally illustrious co-director of the Moscow Art Theater, and the great actors of the day, who were then performing in the Moscow Art Theater repertory. Among the ones we got to know were Leonidov, Moskvin, Kachalov, and Mme. Knipper-Chekhova (the widow of the great Anton Chekhov).

On several afternoons a week we would sit for three or four hours at Stanislavski's side in his studio home while he conducted rehearsals for the Stanislavski Opera, a project which was occupying most of his time during that winter. At night we attended performances of the Moscow Art Theater, and when we had exhausted that repertory we began visiting the other theaters of the rich Russian theatrical season. We saw the performances and met the artists of the Vakhtangov and Maly Theaters and especially of the startling Vsevolod Meyerhold Theater. Some of these men had been students of Stanislavski previously but were now working out their own systems and directing their own companies.

On our first night in Moscow we saw a play directed by Stanislavski himself, and it was an extraordinary surprise to us. The play was *The Marriage of Figaro* by Beaumarchais, and it was done with a racy, intense, farcical spirit which we had not associated with Stanislavski. It was as broad comedy playing and directing as anything we had ever seen. The high-styled members of the cast in flashing colored costumes would run, pose, prance, caress, faint, stutter in confusion, and play out all the intricate patterns of the French farce with a kind of controlled frenzy.

We were stunned. Was this the Stanislavski of the famous method? Was this the work of the great teacher of "affective memory?" It was our first shock at the realization that Stanislavski was a human being—not a distant god—that he was first and foremost the interpreter of the author's play. Up to that minute we had thought of him as a remote philosopher who had envisioned a mystic method of acting. Now we realized he was also a practical man.

In the weeks and months that followed, we saw many plays directed by Stanislavski, including *The Cherry Orchard* with Mme. Chekhova in the leading role and the part originated by Stanislavski now being played by Kachalov. This, of course, was true Stanislavski—moody, thoughtful, and emotional. But it had an underlying earthy humor which was another surprise to us. There were often lusty physical jokes. I can remember Moskvin as Epikhodov watching the departing family talking while he nailed together some crates, his attention so fixed on the touching scene that he was constantly hitting his finger instead of the nail. All through Stanislavski's work there was a strong sense of humor, and it was boldly stated.

On the other hand, *Czar Fyodor Ióannovich* was a pageant. Moskvin played the leading role in a serio-comic way that reminded me often of Chaplin. This pitiful story of the feeble-minded and ineffectual czar even though robed and bejewelled to a dazzling magnificence, was human and tragic, yet always pathetically comic.

*Three Fat Men,* a Stanislavski-supervised Soviet piece, was somewhat in the style of our modern cartoon motion pictures. The three fat men were three actors blown up with papier-mâché and stuffing to resemble three gross caricatures. They represented the Church, Capitalism, and the Army, and it was all done with the exaggerated style of a children's fairy tale.

Such political plays were forced on Stanislavski at the time by a Soviet director who had been assigned to the Moscow Art Theater, and in order to function Stanislavski had to include one Soviet play every so often in the Moscow Art repertoire. Yet each production was produced with the same care and vitality that he gave to the classics.

An outstanding memory to me is the production of Leo Tolstoi's *Resurrection* directed by Nemirovich-Danchenko. Kachalov played the author of the play and walked through the elaborate production speaking the emotions of the actors when they were not speaking themselves. The director took full advantage of the revolving stage at the Moscow Art Theater, and a great deal of the effect of this play was visual. We were impressed by the theatricality of the Moscow Art Theater. We had expected it to be predominantly an actors' theater; instead we found a theater that was shared by the director, the designer, the musician, and above all the author.

In watching Stanislavski rehearse, I saw him making experiments in improvisation. He was directing an opera with young students, and he was trying to break down the cliché gestures and grimaces that had been taught them by singing, dancing, and diction teachers. It was a battle of egos, constant complaining by the actors that they could not sing if they were forced to take this or that position, insistent encouragement from Stanislavski—"Go on! You can do it! Make the tone! Sing!" When the effect had been reached, he was quick to praise.

We asked Stanislavski about the method. "Create your own method," he said to us. "Don't depend slavishly on mine. Make up something that will work for you! But keep breaking traditions, I beg you."

As you can see from reading Mrs. Moore's book, Stanislavski was a complete man of the theater. His teachings encompass voice, diction, dancing, voice tone, singing, make-up, costume, wigs—all the various physical things that would change an actor's shape, form, and size to make him suit his character better.

Mrs. Moore has made a digest in her own words of many of the things Stanislavski talked about and wrote about. It will help actors and students of drama to understand something of Stanislavski's teachings.

Most of all, as Mrs. Moore points out, Stanislavski did not want the method to be an end in itself, but simply a means to an end. It suggests a way of finding personal truth in the creation of a character.

But to enjoy one's creativity to excess, to fall in love with one's inspiration, was farthest from Stanislavski's belief. When I left him that summer he wrote on the photograph he gave me, "Love the art in yourself rather than yourself in the art."

# THE

# STANISLAVSKI

# METHOD

# ONE

# Introduction ▲▲▲▲▲▲▲▲▲▲▲▲▲▲▲▲▲▲▲▲▲▲▲▲

Almost daily one hears or reads about the acting technique known in this country as "the Method," which was developed in Russia by the great actor and director Konstantin S. Stanislavski.

"There were outstanding performances by Method actors." "I am absolutely confused by this famous Method." "Marilyn Monroe studies the Method." "Marlon Brando, Julie Harris, Kim Stanley—Method actors . . ." "John Gielgud studied the Method." "Do not send *me* any of those Method actors. I don't want to be told how to direct." "The Method, I have said, is the grammar of acting."

Such controversial comments make one realize that it is not easy to understand the Method. In the beginning of this century Stanislavski himself had much difficulty in making his "Method" clear to others. Dissatisfied with his own and other Moscow Art Theater actors' performances,

**3**

## The Stanislavski Method

Stanislavski was haunted by a desire to bring the theater out of its stagnant state.

Before Stanislavski was born, Mikhail Shchepkin (1788–1863) had already fought the artificial, declamatory style. This great Russian actor of the Imperial Maly Theater was called the "father of realism" because he was the first to introduce truthful and realistic acting into the Russian theater. Stanislavski, impressed by Shchepkin's teachings and by that actor's brilliant disciple, the actress Glikeria Fedotova, began to work on an acting technique. Stanislavski's concepts were also greatly influenced by the writer Anton Chekhov. The names of these two masters, along with that of the playwright and director Nemirovich-Danchenko, became inseparable from the Moscow Art Theater. Chekhov wrote truthfully about ordinary men and women; he searched for inner beauty in people, and exposed triviality and vice. Under Shchepkin's and Chekhov's influence, artistic simplicity and scenic truth became the foundation of the Stanislavski Method. Mannerisms and clichés were outlawed. For thirty years the object of Stanislavski's study was the creation of an artistically conceived image of life and of a living, truthful human being on the stage.

Watching such great actors as Salvini, Rossi, Duse, Fedotova, Ermolova, and Chaliapin, Stanislavski became aware that when they were at their best they had definite characteristics in common: they were natural and alive on the stage, they gave inspired performances. Stanislavski became certain that an actor was convincing when he existed as a person and did not just pretend to exist. He became conscious that, due probably to the artificial atmosphere of the stage, in front of a mass of people, an actor's senses are often prone to paralysis. An actor loses then the feeling of real life and forgets how to do the simplest things he does naturally and spontaneously in life. Stanislavski realized that an actor has to learn anew to see and not just to pretend to see, to hear and not just to pretend to listen; that he has to talk to his fellow actors and not just to read lines, that he has to think, to feel.

When an actor really sees, hears, and thinks, he *feels* about what he experiences, and his emotions which cannot be reached by forcing come to the surface spontaneously. An actor's intuition then becomes active as in life and helps him to create.

Through tangible, conscious means, the Method teaches an actor to bring himself into a natural, alive state on the stage. But when Stanislavski first read parts of his system to the great Russian actors and to such an eminent theater expert as Prince Sergei Volkonski (author of *The Expressive Word*), for whom Stanislavski had great esteem, they did not understand him. They thought it complicated and boring. "The great rebel," as Maxim Gorki called Stanislavski, encountered strong opposition among his colleagues in the Moscow Art Theater.

In his letters to Lubov Y. Gurevich, a prominent Russian theater historian and critic, Stanislavski said that he was not a writer and that he had no literary ambition. He complained that he did not know how to distribute the enormous amount of his material; "I am drowning in it," he wrote. Is it possible that the manner in which the Stanislavski Method was presented was difficult to understand? How else can it be explained that some of the great actors whose performances were practically the basis from which the Method was developed did not understand it and opposed him?

Nevertheless, several decades ago, when the Method was in its experimental stage, the actors of the Moscow Art Theater became interested in it. They realized that though inspiration for them was almost a normal state on the stage, through the Method they could acquire a technique which consciously led them to it, and they did not have to depend on accident. Eminent actors began to form groups in which they studied the Method.

Since that time, elements of the Method have continually evolved and have been tested as new chemicals are tested in a laboratory. The Method has been proved vital not only for beginners but also for experienced actors. Stanislavski proves that an actor with great talent and subtle means and nuances needs more technique than others, and thus emphasizes his rejection of the widespread layman's opinion that a gifted actor does not need any technique at all.

The Method emerged as a vigorous weapon against overacting, clichés, and mannerisms. It has become a creative technique for the truest portrayal of characters in any play, comedy or tragedy, whether by Chekhov or Ibsen, Shakespeare or O'Neill.

The Method was recognized as a revolutionary theatrical development of great importance and was used even by actors of theaters with entirely different tendencies from those of the Moscow Art Theater. It was known to have been used by the actors of the Russian Meyerhold Theater, whose brilliant director, Vsevolod Meyerhold, left the Moscow Art Theater to experiment on a theatrical revolution of his own, through extreme expressionistic productions. The Method was also studied by the actors of the Kamerny Theater under the direction of the innovator Alexander Tairov. (Tairov's wife, Alice Koonen, a gifted actress with an exceptionally beautiful voice, had left the Moscow Art Theater and become the outstanding actress of the Kamerny Theater, where productions were based on expressiveness of the body and voice.) Some of the actors of the famous old Maly Theater, having practiced the Method, applied for acceptance in the Moscow Art

Theater. Actors became convinced that it brought skill, truth, and life to their performances and to the art of the theater.

One of the reasons for the lack of understanding of the Method in the United States may be the insufficiency of material in English about Stanislavski's conclusions and deductions. Stanislavski himself finished and published only *My Life in Art* and *An Actor Prepares*, the English title of his first book on the Method. (*My Life in Art* was published in 1924 in the United States before it was published in Russia. Stanislavski made changes in this book, considering the original manuscript "too naïve," before publishing it in Russia in 1925.) The book translated into English as *Building a Character* and all other Stanislavski works contain material he had accumulated—sometimes only fragments for future chapters—and were published after his death.

The present controversy about the Method reveals, I am afraid, lack of understanding in those who attack it. The Method is not fiction. "A patient will not get well by reading the prescription. To get well he must take the medicine regularly," said Stanislavski. To be understood, it has to be studied and practiced. Stanislavski saw his Method as a culture which through practice would become second nature to an actor.

The greatest threat to the Method comes, however, not

from its critics but from its adherents. Conversations with young actors and actresses who have studied it make it quite apparent that the Method is not so much misunderstood as simply not understood at all by many.

For instance, very few actors realize that Stanislavski considered creativeness on the stage as the organic blending of psychological and physiological processes. Many "Method actors" completely neglect their physical training. Daily, systematic training in diction, voice, and body was considered by Stanislavski quite as important as practice on inner technique. Real art is a union of the deep substance of inner experience and the vivid outer expression of it. Quality of expressiveness of a performance depends upon such a union; there cannot be true art without it (see Chapter 16).

I heard Stanislavski impress on actors that rehearsals exist for work, for action, and for search of ways to create characters, not for protracted discussion . . . as followers of the Method insist it be today.

Stanislavski also repeated over and over that without great playwrights there would not be theater and that therefore the first duty of the theater is toward the playwright. Moreover, contrary to the distorted understanding of the "Method actor" who harasses the playwright, this duty of the theater to project dynamically the *dramatist's* idea is the foundation of *all* the teachings of Stanislavski.

## The Stanislavski Method

To achieve this goal, actors must create characters as conceived by the author and must create them consciously. Stanislavski rejected mysticism on the stage (see Chapter 12). The lack of understanding of the Method threatens to transform it falsely and eventually to doom it to oblivion.

Stanislavski firmly believed in progress and change; in the hope of finding better and better means to help actors, he was reluctant to write down and set the rules. It may seem presumptuous to attempt to present in brief what took Stanislavski thirty years of meticulous study, research, observation, and experiments to evolve. But the Method is a great contribution, a luminous legacy to the art of the theater, and it is important to me, having studied the Method in a studio of the Moscow Art Theater, to make as clear as I possibly can what Stanislavski, with indomitable logic, sensitive observation, altruistic attitude toward actors, and ardent love for the theater, aspired to achieve.

I was quite young when I won a highly competitive entrance examination to the Studio of the Moscow Art Theater (Vakhtangov Theater) guided and directed by Stanislavski's most celebrated disciple, the brilliant Eugene B. Vakhtangov.

Vakhtangov, said Stanislavski, taught the technique better than he did himself. Every one of this great master Vakhtangov's productions bore his own unique and al-

ways sharp form. And yet Stanislavski's authority was un-
questioned, even for Vakhtangov, who made it a rule to
present all his productions for Stanislavski's approval.
Vakhtangov firmly believed that the actors' education
must be founded on Stanislavski's teachings.

To see such masters at work was truly thrilling. Their
inexhaustible creative source was miraculous. Both were
unconditionally and tirelessly demanding of themselves
and of others in achieving truth on the stage and in creating true characters. Never satisfied, Stanislavski and Vakhtangov were continually striving for better results.

It was understood that everyone in the Moscow Art
Theater and its studios would be present at rehearsals,
whether occupied in them or not. Due to the fact that
Vakhtangov appeared almost every night in a performance, he came to our studio after eleven p.m. and our rehearsals always continued through the night until eight in
the morning. I never missed one of these rehearsals during
the years I was in the Studio of the Moscow Art Theater.
Even in my young years I was interested mostly in direction.

Besides being unique as directors, Stanislavski and
Vakhtangov possessed great talent as actors. Blessed with
the gifts of exceptional imagination and impetuous artistic
temperament, they often included themselves as characters in a rehearsal. Such a performance carried the actors

away, stimulating them and giving them a more thorough understanding of the characters.

In addition to watching Stanislavski as a genius, we were always witnesses of his great humanity. I shall never forget the occasion when he came to our theater for the preview of Vakhtangov's masterpiece, *Princess Turandot.* Vakhtangov himself was in bed, at home, mortally ill.

Though our theater was filled with important theatrical personalities, during the intermission Stanislavski went to Vakhtangov's house to congratulate him. Nikolai M. Gorchakov, one of the actors of our studio, now a director and important as a writer on the theater, accompanied Stanislavski that evening. He later recounted the scene. Stanislavski had told Vakhtangov that his production was magnificent and unusual, demonstrating genius and originality.

"But still, I want my actors to live truthfully—to really laugh and cry. Do you believe the actors in *Turandot?*" asked Vakhtangov.

"You achieved a miracle today. You conquered us," answered Stanislavski.

Stanislavski returned to the theater and the performance of *Turandot* resumed.

When our studio played *Turandot* in the Moscow Art Theater itself, I was awed by the atmosphere there. I remember Stanislavski's coming backstage for the express purpose of encouraging the young actors and actresses. His majestic presence added excitement. His genius, his humanity, and his love for the art of the theater imbued the walls and the air around us.

Though Stanislavski used to rehearse a play for several months, his technique, if understood, will prove extremely useful in the American theater, where a play is rehearsed for only a few weeks. The Method teaches an actor the shortest way to accomplish what the director demands of him. In a theater where the director on occasion has time only to demand results, knowing how to achieve these quickly and effectively is especially valuable.

It is indisputable that there is a great deal of dilettantism in the theater. Stanislavski fights this dillettantism through the Method. He considers even an accidental inspiration a form of dilettantism. His Method teaches *professionalism* in the theater, and through professionalism theater becomes art.

It should, however, be well understood that the Method is not a dogma to be followed literally or pedantically. With it Stanislavski intended only to indicate the right road to actors and directors: "Today the best means is . . . ; tomorrow we shall find a more perfect one," he said. Stanislavski warned against allowing the Method to become an end in itself, a dogma which would destroy the actor's creative process. The fact that he continually changed and innovated the technique proves that he would not stop doing so if he were alive.

# TWO

# Art of the Theater ~~~~~~~~~~~~~

*"The theater infects the audience with its noble
ecstasy."*

—K. S. Stanislavski

It is the artistic quality of the actor's performance, the
quality of the atmosphere backstage as well as on stage,
the artistic discipline, the sense of responsibility, and the
creative attitude of all those participating in giving birth
to a performance, of every actor and of every stage hand,
which, when united, create the vibrant anticipation in the
audience.

The art of the theater is based on collective work,
and it is essential that everyone in a group work for the
benefit of the whole performance and not solely for himself. Ethics, high morale, and stern discipline are indispen-
sable in such a group. Reproduction of life on the stage is

for the actors both a challenge and a responsibility toward the people who come to see it. An actor's exciting profession is one of responsibility because it is the actor who breathes life into a written play. It is he who makes the play tangible, alive, valid, and exciting.

Stanislavski believed that life artistically re-created on the stage becomes superior entertainment, and that superior entertainment is educational. Therefore an actor spreads culture and his profession has dignity; he has a right to be proud of it. He respects his profession and makes others respect it.

The widespread opinion that the actor's work is something mysterious that cannot be learned consciously was considered by Stanislavski a prejudice and, like all prejudices, harmful to culture and progress. He thought it an alibi for the laziness of an actor's thought and for dilettantism in the theater. His Method is a conscious professional approach to the theater, and when it is mastered it gives an actor exceptional possibilities for achieving artistic results in the field of dramatic creativeness.

It is useless for an actor to sit and wait for inspiration to descend upon him every time he has to perform. Inspiration alone will not make up for skill. If inspiration refuses to "descend," through skill an actor can give a good, if not inspired, performance. But without inspiration *or* skill an actor will give a disastrous performance.

One of the greatest geniuses in the Russian Theater,
Eugene B. Vakhtangov, said that inspiration will come to
an actor with the certainty that he has his will under control, with the sureness that he has a responsive body and a
trained voice, with his knowledge of the laws of technique,
with his pride in his profession and his joy in every minute
of performing or rehearsing. This knowledge will also add
to an actor's dignity and to his modesty. And by coming
on the stage prepared he proves his respect for his audience.

The really great artists are those who are able to unite
inspiration and hard work. It is a misconception to think
that gifted actors never work. Every biography of great
actors proves the contrary; they never stopped searching
for a conscious technique and they continually worked on
every inner and outer motion, on the mastery of every
word which makes theater the strongest expression of the
creative arts.

The great Italian actress Eleonora Duse was known as
a hard worker. Talma, the famous French actor of the
eighteenth century, said that an actor needs twenty years
to master his profession. And the celebrated nineteenth-
century Russian actress Glikeria Fedotova said that actors
were wasting their time waiting for the god Apollo to send
them inspiration from heaven. Apollo was too busy with
his own affairs! she said, and she advised actors to work

hard to be able to evoke inspiration. She was taught and coached by Mikhail Shchepkin, and she recommended that actors seek help from other experienced artists. Stanislavski himself was sometimes coached by his brilliant disciple Vakhtangov.

Theater, being the artistic re-creation of life, according to Stanislavski, has life's great problem: the moments passed on the stage cannot be repeated, as spent moments in real life cannot be brought back. When actors try to repeat what they did the night before, the theater stops being art because it stops being living theater. Every performance in a living theater is as different as all days are different, but in order that the theater should be living, there must be living people on the stage.

The Method will teach actors to function on the stage automatically as live human beings. In mastering this technique, actors will not have to depend on chance. For chance, as every artist knows, is the enemy of art.

# THREE

# The Method ▲▲▲▲▲▲▲▲▲▲▲▲▲▲▲▲▲▲▲▲▲▲▲▲▲▲

*"There are no small parts, only small actors."*
—Motto for the Moscow Art Theater

*"The difficult must become habit, habit easy, and the easy beautiful."*
—Prince Sergei Volkonski

*"Most important: create consciously and truthfully."*
—Mikhail Shchepkin

*"There is no Stanislavski system. . . . There is only the authentic incontestable one—the system of nature itself."*
—K. S. Stanislavski

# 1 ACTION, ''IF,'' ''GIVEN CIRCUMSTANCES''

The word "drama" comes from the ancient Greek word meaning "to do," "to act," and such words as "activity," "act," "actor" are related to the Latin word *actio*, which means an action taking place on the stage. Like everything that takes place in real life, everything that takes place on the stage is a form of activity. When an actor is on the stage he must be *active*.

To be active does not necessarily mean to be active externally or physically. One can be immobile externally yet active psychologically, having inner action. It is important on the stage to be absorbed in inner activity. Sometimes the external immobility may even be an expression of extreme inner activity. For instance, upon hearing tragic news, a person may remain still while extremely intense inwardly.

On the stage there must always be inner or external action or both. And these actions—everything an actor does on the stage—must be justified, must have a purpose and be logical.

# The Stanislavski Method

For instance, in executing the physical act of closing a door, the actor must have a motive; he may want it closed to stop a draft, or because he does not want people in the next room to hear what he is saying. An actor must do it for his own purpose and not merely to demonstrate to the audience that he is closing a door. The physical act of closing a door is the result of his inner reason and therefore justified. Logic, concreteness, and consecutiveness will make the physical action truthful and believable. If an actor executes it fully, thoroughly, and precisely, he will feel as comfortable as if he were doing it in real life. He then does it consciously and will feel about what he is doing. If he performs a truthful, logical physical action it becomes organic, that is, natural and spontaneous, and this gives birth to the emotion. If he forces an emotion, he only locks it up and forgets about his actions.

A simple, truthfully executed physical action is the first and most effective means of making an actor's faculties function and of involving his emotions.

### EXERCISES* FOR ACTION

1. Sit, stand, walk. Justify everything you do. For example, sit at a window in order to see what is happening in the house opposite you; sit in order to rest.

2. Stand to be photographed; stand in order to see better.

* Not all the examples for exercises in this text are Stanislavski's. He encouraged actors and students of drama to invent their own.

3. Walk to pass time; walk to annoy the people who live in an apartment below.

4. Clean your bureau drawers.

5. Count the number of objects on the table.

### Improvisations

1. You have to leave school because you cannot afford to pay tuition. A friend wants to help you but she has no money. She brings you a valuable brooch. You refuse the gift but your friend insists, lays it on a dresser, and leaves. You take your friend to the entrance door. When you come back, the pin has disappeared. Can anyone have taken it while you were out of the room?

Do not think about your emotions. An emotion is a result of an experience. If what you are doing is justified and you are fully concentrating upon it, you will feel about what you do and about what you experience and your emotions will appear spontaneously.

2. Burn a letter. First, think what you would do before burning it. You may want to read it again; you may hesitate to destroy it. Think what you would do if you were sitting at a real fireplace.

Think of your objective, not of your feelings. You will feel at ease and relaxed if you concentrate on it. Do not try too hard, but do not be nonchalant in executing your action. Be concrete in what you are doing. Do not do anything "in general." " 'In general,' " said Stanislavski, "is the enemy of art."

23

Through the word *if* which Stanislavski calls "magic" or "creative," you will create for yourself problems to be solved. Striving to solve them will naturally lead you to inner and external actions.

*If* carries the actor out of real life into imaginary circumstances. This little word starts creativeness. An actor must ask himself what he would do *if* he were in such a situation and try to answer this question explicitly and precisely. By asking, "What would I do *if* I were . . . ?" an actor does not have to force himself to believe that he *is* such a person in such circumstances. "If" is a supposition and it does not imply or assert anything that exists. It helps one to think of something that *could* exist.

*If* stimulates true *inner activity* because an actor, by asking what he himself would do, stimulates his own emotions, and brings himself into the imaginary circumstances of the character he is portraying.

*If* is a powerful stimulus to the imagination, thoughts, and emotions. An actor must go through the whole part using this "magic *if*." It will bring him into an inner-functioning creative state.*

---

* Stanislavski wrote in one of his letters to Lubov Y. Gurevich that in 1931 Charles Chaplin had written in an article that he was using "if" for all his creative work.

24

The Method

**EXERCISES FOR ''IF''**

1. You are dressing for an important reception. What would you do *if* the lights suddenly went out?

2. You have come to see your sick friend. What would you do *if* in his house you met a person you had not seen in a long time because you consider him your enemy?

3. You have made all the preparations to go on vacation (tickets, hotels, and so on). What would you do *if* someone at your office called and told you that you must postpone the vacation?

4. Think for a moment that here, where you are working, there once lived a man who lost his mind and became a dangerous lunatic. What would you do *if* you learned that he had escaped from the asylum and was behind this door?


*Given circumstances* are the plot of the play, the events, the epoch, the time and place of the action, the conditions of life, the director's and the actors' interpretation, the setting, properties, lighting, sound effects, and so on—all the circumstances which an actor encounters while he creates a role.

An actor must become familiar with environment—"given circumstances"—to such an extent that he becomes a part of it. If he succeeds in it, his true emotions will respond.

## EXERCISES FOR "GIVEN CIRCUMSTANCES"

Execute justified actions under various given circumstances:

1. Put on a new shirt to go to a dance on a ship. Put on a clean shirt after a day's work in a mine.

2. Pack to go on vacation; to leave for the war.

3. Enter your apartment at night, after a party. Enter your office in the morning.

4. You arrive in Paris; come back to New York.

5. Furnish the room in which you are going to play an exercise. It will have a psychological effect and help you to feel at ease. In every exercise think of your objective.

# 2 IMAGINATION

The task of an actor and of his creative technique is to transform the story of the play into an artistic, scenic reality. Since the imagination plays a dominant role in such a transformation, an actor must be sure that his imagination functions properly. It must be cultivated and developed; it must be alert, rich, and active. An actor must learn to think on any theme. He must observe people, their behavior, try to understand their mentality. He must be sure to notice what is around him. He must learn to compare. He must learn to dream and with his inside vision create scenes and take part in them.

A playwright rarely describes the past or the future and even omits many details of the present life of his characters. An actor must complete his biography in his mind from beginning to end, because knowing how the character grew up, what influenced his behavior, and what he expects his future to be will give more substance to the present life of the character and will give the actor a perspective and a feeling of movement in the role. If an actor does not fill in all these missing events and movements, the life he portrays will not be complete.

An artistic, rich imagination will also contribute a great deal when an actor interprets the lines and fills them with the meaning that lies behind, the "subtext." The lines of the author are dead until an actor analyzes and brings out the sense which the author intended to give to them. A simple phrase such as "I have a headache" may have various meanings; the person who says it may be afraid that the headache is a symptom of a serious illness; he may want a pretext to go away; he may be hinting to guests who will not leave. Important are the meaning, the thoughts, and the intention—not simply the words. If an actor with the help of his imagination finds interesting meaning behind the words, his intonations also will be expressive and interesting. He will then transmit images to his fellow actors and not just read lines. "Speak to the eye, not to the ear," said Mikhail Shchepkin. "Spectators come to the theater to hear the subtext; the text they can read at home," said Stanislavski.

Everything you imagine must be precise and logical. Always know who you are, when your imaginary scene is happening, where, how, why, and what for. All this will help you to have a definite picture of an imaginary life. Even if you try to live the life of an inanimate object, you can stir inner activity if you ask yourself, and answer with the help of your imagination: who, when, where, why, how, and what for? When an actor is carried away by his creative imagination, he is active naturally and spontaneously, and this awakens his emotions.

Every word and movement of an actor on the stage must be the result of a well-functioning imagination. Exercises will help to make the imagination active, strong, and rich.

**EXERCISES**

1. In your mind, go through your walk from class to home; imagine being at home, cleaning your room.

Follow your logic and closely watch the work of your imagination. Gradually you will stop being an observer and merge with the "you" you are watching. You will be in the state which Stanislavski calls "I am," which means "I live," "I exist."

2. When asked a simple question, such as, "Is it cold today?" or "Did you enjoy the party yesterday?" glance back quickly in your imagination, remember how the people you met in the street were dressed or what happened at the party, and then answer.

3. Look at a picture of an unknown person. Tell who this could be. Try to guess the person's profession, what his family could be like, what his tastes are; learn to judge from his costume, eyes, hair-do, and so on.

4. In your imagination, go around the world.

Do not imagine anything vaguely or halfway. Use all possible concrete, consecutive details. Logic and proper sequence will make what you imagine real. As you work on a role, your words will become your own when you have your own vision, your own picture of the event and the people. You have to achieve a continuous, logical chain of images in your mind, related to the given circumstances of the exercise. These images will stir your inner life and evoke your emotions.

29

**Improvisation**

Play an episode which happens to members of a scientific expedition. Their plane is out of order. Decide where the forced landing takes place. Use your imagination to develop this accident in the greatest possible detail.

# 3 CONCENTRATION OF ATTENTION ON THE STAGE

Several decades ago, when actors of the Moscow Art Theater began to study the Method, they used to spend ten or fifteen minutes in complete silence in order to concentrate. A well-known actress used to put a shawl on her head and no one dared to approach her lest he interfere with her "concentration." Later this unhealthy attitude changed and many actors deliberately spoke of matters not related to the performance. They proved that with practice they could concentrate at will on any object.

In order to keep his attention from wandering to the audience, an actor must interest himself in what is happening on the stage. It is impossible to forget the audience completely. To try to force oneself into believing that one is alone, that one does not see anybody or hear anything in the audience would also be contradictory to the art of the theater. But it is possible for an actor to be without fear, to feel at ease, and to achieve on the stage what Stanislavski calls *public solitude,* if his attention is concentrated on physical or psychological tasks. A concrete thought or a concrete action will hold an actor's attention.

On the stage an actor has to learn anew to see and hear, because in front of an audience his natural faculties are often prone to paralysis. Actors frequently only pretend that they see or hear. To be a live human being on the stage, an actor's faculties must function as they do in life. An actor's eye that really sees attracts the spectator's attention and directs it where he wants. An actor's eye which does not see takes the spectator's attention away from the stage.

An actor can make himself actually see anything on the stage—a vase, a picture, a book—by building around it some imaginary details which will make it attractive to him. The more an actor exercises his concentration, the sooner it will become automatic; finally it will become second nature to him.

In the beginning of this training, it is necessary to practice with an object nearby. The actor must examine it in every detail. He must be relaxed and not make too great an effort. It is his imagination, not his body, that must make the effort to see. There must be no physical tension while he is concentrating his attention on the object. An inexperienced actor always feels that he does not *give* enough. "Cut ninety-five per cent," says Stanislavski. An actor need not try to amuse the audience. If with the help of his imagination he sees the object and is interested in it, the audience will also be interested.

Besides single objects of attention there are what Stanislavski calls *circles of attention,* in which an actor must learn to concentrate.

A *small circle of attention* is a small area which includes the actor and, perhaps, a nearby table with a few things on it. The actor is the center of such a small area and can easily have his attention absorbed by the objects inside it.

The *medium circle of attention* is an area which may include several persons and groups of furniture. An actor should examine this gradually, not trying to take it in all at once.

The *large circle of attention* is everything an actor can see on the stage. The larger the circle of attention, the more difficult it is to keep the attention from dissipating.

When an actor feels that his attention is wandering, he should immediately direct it to a single object and concentrate on that. When he succeeds and surmounts the difficulty, he can redirect his attention first to a small circle, then to a medium one, and then to a large one.

As well as learning to concentrate on things he sees on the stage, an actor must learn to concentrate on sounds he hears and on objects in his mind. When an actor succeeds in concentrating on an inner or external object, his inner life will respond and his emotions will appear.

### EXERCISES

1. Examine any object that is close. Notice its form, lines, color, and any other possible details. Without looking at it, tell what you remember. Gradually cut down the time allowed for absorbing the object. Do the same with an object at a moderate distance; with one far away.

Attention tends to dissipate when you try to concentrate on distant objects. To build an imaginary story about them will be of great value in controlling your attention. For instance, look at a cup; think that Napoleon drank from it. Look at the rug under your feet; think that it was in the palace of a Turkish sultan, in a harem.

2. Listen to the sounds in the street. Tell what you hear.

3. Concentrate on one object. Gradually direct your attention to the small, to the medium, and to the large circles of attention and back to the object.

Exercises strengthen an actor's ability and help to make his attention sharp and strong. To develop concentration, an actor may use the same exercises he uses to develop his imagination.

## The Stanislavski Method

Observe people and nature. Enrich your inner impressions with music, paintings, literature. Penetrate into a person's inner world. Try to understand the reasons for his behavior. Practice this in life and do it on the stage. If you concentrate sharply, your emotions will respond.

As a theme for practicing concentration, Stanislavski offers the following melodramatic plot.

**Improvisation**

A husband is counting money that he could not deposit in the bank because of the lateness of the hour. The money is not his; it belongs to the company for which he works. His wife, in the adjoining room, is bathing their new-born baby. Watching the husband as he takes the bands off the paper and throws them into the burning fireplace is his brother-in-law, a hunchback and a half-wit. The wife calls her husband. After he goes into the adjoining room, the half-wit imitates his motions, but throws the money instead of the bands into the fireplace. The husband returns in time to see the last pack of money burning. He screams and pushes his brother-in-law, who falls and hits his temple against the andiron. The wife hears the screams and runs in. She asks her husband to bring water to wash the blood from her brother's head. But the husband is in a state of shock and does not understand anything. She runs out to get water and a scream is heard. Her baby has drowned while she was away.

An actor will not overact even in this melodrama if he strives to execute all his actions with maximum truthfulness. In striving to achieve such truthfulness in his physical and inner actions, an actor's attention will be fully concentrated on what he is doing on the stage.

Start your work on this scene using the "magic *if.*"

# 4 RELAXATION OF THE MUSCLES

Believing relaxation of the muscles fundamental to an actor's inner training, Stanislavski included this element in his first book on the inner technique instead of presenting it in a later work devoted to an actor's physical means of expression. Stanislavski emphatically proved that unless tense muscles are relaxed an actor's normal mental activity, and therefore the spiritual life of the character he portrays, is impossible. Thus an actor must have control over his muscles.

It is impossible and therefore unnecessary to try to relax all the muscles. Those which participate directly in a given pose or movement have to be appropriately tense; but even the slightest tension of other muscles can bring paralysis to an actor's creative state.

Almost every time an actor appears before an audience,

**35**

his muscles are tense and he must know how to cope with them. He must control this tension constantly. Through systematic work he will develop an "observer" inside himself. The "observer" will watch and instantly find the spot of unnecessary tension and as instantly eliminate it. This will become a mechanical, normal habit.

#### EXERCISES

1. Take any position—lying, sitting, or standing. Note the muscles which are not involved in the pose and are unnecessarily tense; relax them.

2. Bring groups of muscles to maximum tension. Relax them. You will become familiar with your muscles and it will be easy to subordinate them.

3. Justify your pose. You will note that it is easier to relax your muscles when doing so. Use the "magic *if*" and "given circumstances" for your justification. The pose will then stop being just a pose. It will have a purpose and become active. For instance, raise your arm and ask yourself what you would do if you were in a garden and would like to pick a peach from a tree. Because you have a motive and a purpose, your pose will become alive, and superfluous tension will disappear more easily.

Concentration on a concrete thought or a concrete action will help you to relax.

While practicing, remember three points: tension, relaxation, justification.

# 5 UNITS AND OBJECTIVES

In order to build a logical, consecutive performance and to assimilate his role, an actor must break it up into separate units. This will also be exceptionally helpful in memorizing the part.

As has been said in the chapter on action, an actor on the stage must always carry out physical or psychological actions or both; usually physical and psychological (inner) actions are interwoven. Inner action is the *objective* which an actor must fulfill in order to convey it to the audience. He must remember that his reason for being on stage is the conveying of his objective to the audience.

A *unit* is a section of a role between two different objectives; it ends when an actor completes one *objective;* a new unit starts with a new objective. For example, a friend comes to help a married couple to settle a difference. His objective in such a unit is to *help*. After he fulfills this objective, he takes leave, trying to hide the fact that he

**37**

himself is in love with his friend's wife and that he will never see them again. This will be a new unit because the actor will have another objective to fulfill: to *hide* an emotion.

After an actor has divided his role into such units, he may break each one into smaller "beats" with various objectives. For instance, in trying to *help* he may want to *convince* the husband to pay more attention to his wife, he may *reproach* the young wife for not being serious enough about her duties, and so on. Playing the smaller beats and energetically striving to fulfill each of the objectives will add color and variety to the larger unit.

For many years Stanislavski taught and applied this breaking up of a play into units, analyzing and discovering the units' objectives by having the director and the actors sit around a table with their scripts and pencils. He loved this preparatory period, which preceded rehearsals and which lasted a very long time.

In the last years of his directorial and pedagogical career, Stanislavski changed this practice. Experience proved that to understand what an actor must convey was much easier during rehearsals than while sitting around the table, so Stanislavski started rehearsals almost immediately. This new approach saved time and the productions were staged much faster.

As an actor's role matures he will not have to think of smaller beats. They will blend into the larger unit, leaving the color and variety of all the possible characteristic details of a given moment.

In order to understand what his objective at a given moment is, an actor must analyze the essence of a unit. An objective is the inner action, the central important point around which the unit is built.

Units and objectives must be strongly related to the *main idea* of the author of the play. An actor must not forget that his first duty is to convey the main idea. Everything he does on the stage must contribute to this.

Striving to accomplish the objective of a unit gives an actor reasons for his activity analogous, of course, to the activity of the character he portrays. If he energetically strives to carry out his objective, an actor will convey it to his audience; his natural faculties will function, his emotions will be involved, and his intuition will help his creative process.

As a typical example of an objective which is an inner action interwoven with a physical action, Stanislavski cites one from a scene in Pushkin's *Mozart and Salieri*. Salieri, uncontrollably jealous of Mozart, whose music he admires, decides to kill him. He must take a glass, pour wine, and put poison into it. Though these are physical actions they are full of psychological meaning. They may be called psychological actions which have a physical element.

In executing an objective, an actor should give maximum attention to the physical actions in it, because this will prevent the forcing of emotions and will naturally bring the actor into the right psychological state.

In order to remember easily what a unit is about, an actor must find a name for it which will characterize its inner meaning and will instantly give him a clear idea of the essence of the unit; this name may be a noun.

To define an objective, an active verb should be used; it should express precisely and logically the end an actor wants to achieve. Often an actor can add impetus to the carrying out of his objective by adding "I wish" to the name he has found for his unit. For instance, if the name of a unit is "freedom," he can convert it to "I wish freedom" as the name for his objective. If, in the process of his work on a role, an actor feels that he should change his objective, he must do so.

There is usually in each unit something that opposes the carrying out of the unit's objective. For instance, in the example offered above (the friend who came to help settle the difference between a husband and wife), the "counter-action" may be the fact of the friend's love for the young woman. Striving honestly to help the marriage, he must overcome his own feelings. There may be other obstacles, such as the husband who might not want to listen to his well-meaning friend. Overcoming such obstacles keeps an actor from becoming nonchalant and forces him to carry out his inner action more vividly, with more energy and strength. The actor himself should imagine more obstacles, justified, of course, by his role.

# 6 FEELING OF TRUTH AND BELIEF

*Truth* on the stage is different from truth in life. In a play there are no true facts or true events; everything is invention. To *believe* on the stage does not mean that an actor must practice self-hypnosis or force himself to have hallucinations. It means that an actor treats things or persons as if they were what he wants the audience to believe they are. An actor knows that his fellow actor is not his father or an emperor, but he can treat him as his

41

father or as an emperor. He can treat an object as if it were a fluttering bird. The ability of an actor to make his audience believe what he wants it to believe creates scenic truth. The moments in which he succeeds in this constitute art on the stage.

If an actor while carrying out an action uses logical consecutiveness, justifies everything with the help of *if*, and thinks of the *given circumstances*, he will not overact and his action will be truthful. Without forcing himself, he will believe in what he is doing because he will be doing it as in real life. Physical actions without the help of any objects ("with air") develop an actor's concentration, imagination, feeling of truth and belief, feeling of the right measure. Such exercises teach an actor to achieve the maximum of truthfulness in his actions.

A well-executed action can be of exceptional help to an actor during tragic moments in a play. While an inner tragic action may lead him to overact and to force his emotions, a truthfully executed simple physical action related to and justified by the given moment will make his faculties function: his truthful emotions in the given circumstances will appear spontaneously and he will be introduced naturally into the inner experience of the character he portrays.

When an actor brings everything he does to the maximum of truthfulness and feels as if he were doing it in real life, he enters a state of *I am,* where he exists, he lives and is blending with his role.

Truth and belief are forceful and effective stimuli to an actor's emotions. But in trying to make his actions truthful, an actor must avoid clichés and remember that there are varieties of truth. There is uninteresting truth as well as interesting and unusual truth. In executing his actions, inner or physical, an actor must always look for the unexpected and the true at the same time. His actions must be free from unattractive everyday details. They must be real but artistic, in good taste.

To find such unusual forms of truth, an actor must see, watch, absorb all possible impressions around him. An actor must learn to be aware of what surrounds him.

#### EXERCISES

1. Dress and undress without using any properties, while changing the given circumstances; for instance, dress for work, for a party. Undress at home; in a hospital before an operation.

Remember and execute every typical characteristic and real detail. Bring each little action to the very limit of truthfulness and you will feel comfortable as if you were doing it in life.

To make those who watch you believe in what you are doing, you must achieve perfection in your actions. The exercises will teach you to do every physical action precisely, clearly, and logically.

2. Execute a series of only physical actions from your role or your improvisation. Repeat them until you have fixed the physical path of the role.

By executing separate moments as a whole uninterrupted sequence of justified truthful actions, you build the physical life of the character you portray. Giving life to the body stirs the inner spiritual life of your role.

3. Stab yourself with a paper cutter. Treat it as if it were a sword.

Do not exaggerate the truth and do not indulge in naturalism. In every exercise use your logic, common sense, and taste to check the proportion and measure of truthfulness.

# 7 EMOTIONAL MEMORY

During the last years of his career, Stanislavski almost completely abandoned his means of stimulating the actor's emotions through the memory of experienced ones. Practice convinced him that the indirect approach to stirring emotions with the help of a precise, strongly logical action will infallibly make an actor's senses function. When his senses function, the actor is in an inner creative state and his emotions appear naturally.

Actions always involve the psychological and physical life of a person. But since physical actions can be controlled more easily than psychological ones, which are intangible, an actor should bring to perfection the physical actions of his role. These will stir his psychological life, give him better understanding of the play and of his character, and evoke in him feelings analogous to it. To achieve logic, precision, and consecutiveness in an action, Stanislavski recommends exercises to be carried out without the help of any objects ("with air") as described in Chapter 6.

Starting rehearsals of Molière's *Tartuffe* and working with the actors of the Moscow Art Theater on the basis of the last developments of his system, Stanislavski said to them, "I am not going to live long.* It is my duty to transmit to actors my experience and my knowledge. Learn to carry out correctly and organically the simplest physical actions. The logic and consecutiveness in these actions will evoke in you the entire complicated subtle scale of inner experiences. Carrying out the logic of a physical action will bring you to the logic of feelings, and this is everything for an actor."

* Rehearsals of *Tartuffe* were interrupted by Stanislavski's death.

## The Stanislavski Method

Because many actors still practice the approach to emotions through "emotional memory" and because Stanislavski did not entirely reject it, the use of emotional memory is described below.

Stanislavski was continually seeking to increase his knowledge of all the facets of human inner life. He studied psychology, physiology, aesthetics as well as historical and theoretical writings of the theater. He met and had conferences with scientists and intellectuals of various specialized fields.*

Stanislavski was interested in experimental psychology and especially in the works of the famous French psychologist Ribot, whose term *affective memory* he used. Later, in the 1930s, he rejected this name and replaced it by *emotional memory*.

Emotional memory brings back our past experiences and emotions and makes us relive them. We can also relive sensations experienced through our five senses. For instance, through visual memory we can actually see a per-

* After Stanislavski's system became recognized in Russia, it had followers not only among actors but also among persons who had no direct relation to the theater. It was taught by psychologists and even by doctors. Many of these persons had no idea how to teach it and gave it a very vague, often mystical character: concentration, relaxation, belief became important in their own right. Actors were torturing themselves studying with such "teachers." This was not what Stanislavski taught; he intended his system only as a means to help actors. Later Stanislavski abandoned some of the teachings which contributed to this unhealthy attitude.

son we may have forgotten, a landscape or an object we have once seen. Through our sound memory we can hear music once heard, or voices of people we once knew. Smell, taste, and touch can bring back sensations once experienced. The memory of sensations has great influence on our emotional memory. A perfume may bring back the memory of a person who used it; it may recall a series of emotions experienced in connection with that person. The taste of a certain food can bring back the memory of a party, its whole atmosphere, the emotions experienced there.

Through his emotional memory an actor evokes his own emotions, which must be analogous to those of his role. An actor must always stir his own emotions if he does not want to force and to overact but wants to create a living human being on the stage. An actor himself, in different given circumstances, with different objectives for each role, is the best material for creating a new life on the stage. A human being is a reservoir of innumerable moods, states, experiences, and emotions, and an actor must bring out and use the ones that are typical of the role.

To be efficient the emotional memory must be exercised, and, though every person has a reservoir of past experiences and memories, the actor must continue to enrich his. He must observe what is happening around him; he must read, listen to music, go to museums, watch people. If an

**47**

actor understands people's behavior, their mentality and mannerisms, he may be able to make them his own and use them for a role in an analogous situation. His own emotions will also respond if he sympathizes with another person. An effort of will and mind will make emotional memory function, and this will arouse true and spontaneous emotions.

An emotion which appears at a moment of inspiration may not come again. An actor must think and analyze in order to discover what stimulus has awakened it. The next time he performs, he should go back to the stimulus and use it to stir the emotion anew. Remember that an emotion is always the result of an experience. "Emotion is like a flower. Once withered you cannot revive it. But water the roots and you will have a fresh one," said Mikhail Shchepkin.

To stir emotions, all possible stimuli should be used:

1. Logical, consecutive and truthful physical and inner actions.
2. The *magic if* and the *given circumstances*.
3. Imagination.
4. Concentration of attention on objects.
5. Units and objectives.
6. Truth and Belief.
7. The subtext (the meaning behind the lines in a play).

8. The interrelationship between characters in the play.

9. Lighting, sound effects, *mise en scène*, everything that creates the illusion of life on the stage.

These stimuli are the psycho-technical elements. If an actor learns to use these conscious means, each of them will become a stimulus to his emotions.

### EXERCISES

The atmosphere around us influences our emotions on the stage as it does in real life. The right *mise en scène* and lighting influence the actor's emotional memory. And sometimes, by following his mood and his objective, an actor finds the right *mise en scène;* each must have a psychological justification. A *mise en scène* must bring out the inner experience in an impressive form.

1. Form a group at a table. Of what does this particular *mise en scène* remind you?

2. Listen to sounds from the street. What does the sound of the siren bring to your memory? Build a *mise en scène* appropriate to your mood.

3. Turn off some of the lights. Of what does this semi-dark room remind you?

Create a *mise en scène* that is the result of your inner actions, thoughts, and emotions.

Preparing the setting yourself will help you enter the ground and actions of your character.

**49**

# 8 COMMUNION

To be in communion with another person on the stage means to be aware of this person's presence, to make sure that he hears and understands what you tell him and that you hear and understand what he tells you. Through an active transmission of his lines, an actor will impress on his fellow actor what he wants him to see and to hear. If he energetically communicates to the other actor his thoughts and experiences, analogous to those of his role, he will be carried away and will merge with the character he is portraying. If he communicates with determination, even a bad actor will respond. An actor must absorb what the other person tells him. The words and the thoughts of others must come to an actor as if he were hearing them for the first time. The communion must be reciprocal and should not be interrupted when another actor speaks. It should not be interrupted during silences or pauses if an actor wants that life on the stage to be continuous.*

Sometimes an actor talks to himself on the stage. Without offering this as a part of his Method, Stanislavski describes how he himself behaved "to be in correct communion with himself." He made the brain and the solar plexus, which are two centers of our nerves' life, "talk" to each other. He felt as if he had two I's, which established a steady dialogue between themselves as if they were two actors.

To communicate with an imaginary object (for instance, the ghost of Hamlet's father), an actor must use the "magic if" and tell himself honestly what he would do *if* he saw a ghost.

An actor should never practice without another person, because he might become accustomed to receiving no reaction and would have difficulty in communicating on the stage with a person who does react and respond.

An actor must also be aware of inanimate objects on the stage.

Communion with the audience takes place only indirectly through communion between actors, unless other-

* In the early period of the use of the Method, communion on the stage was taught through "giving out and receiving rays of invisible spiritual currents." This was abandoned by Stanislavski because such mutual hypnotism did not always bring the desired results; on the contrary, the actor's muscles sometimes became extremely tense through striving for "spiritual rays," and hampered every physical and inner activity.

wise required by the style of the theatrical work, as, for example, in *commedia dell' arte.*

In mass scenes an actor communicates with different people in the crowd. He may be in communion with one person or with all of them. Stanislavski demanded from every actor—not alone from the principals but even from those who took part only in the mass scenes—a detailed biography of the character they were portraying. Actors without a single word to say created characters full of inner content and brought individual lives to the stage.

An honest unbroken communion between actors keeps the audience's attention and makes them part of what takes place on the stage.

The alert, sharp use of an actor's senses is necessary in order to achieve a strong communion. When an actor without any physical tension sees intensely, hears intensely, and so on, he has a complete "grasp."

### EXERCISES

1. Attract the attention of your fellow actor; make him be aware of you. Use any possible means: surprise him, greet him, entertain him, humiliate him, embarrass him.

2. Be well aware of your fellow actor's personality. Try to understand the reasons for his behavior. Try to understand what he tries to tell you.

# 9 ADAPTATION

Adaptation is an exceptionally effective means of communion between actors on the stage. To adjust oneself to another, one must be well aware of that person's presence and personality. For example: You have an important appointment at five o'clock. It is four-forty-five and your employer is still dictating to you in his office. Find a way to leave and to be on time for your appointment.

The necessity for evaluating the circumstances in relation to your employer, for inventing an ingenious reason to leave and to be on time for the appointment, means to find an adjustment for the situation.

Actors must adjust to one another on the stage, as people in life do when they meet. A human being's behavior depends on his relationship with other people around him. This law must be the basis of every scenic action. If you talk to a stupid person you will try to adjust to his mentality and talk simply in order to be understood by him. If you are with a shrewd person you have to act cautiously and look for subtle adaptations so that he does not see through you and does not guess what you have in mind.

New conditions of life, a new atmosphere, a new place, the time of day or night—all require appropriate adaptation. People behave differently at night and during the day. In a foreign country one adjusts oneself to the local conditions. The quality and variety of adaptation is extremely important on the stage. To be interesting, an adaptation must be strong, sharp, imaginative, unexpected, and in good taste. It must be personal—the actor's own— and therefore original.

An unexpected adaptation is always impressive. For instance, if according to what is happening on the stage the audience expects an actor to scream at another actor, but instead of screaming he speaks softly, this is unexpected and can be impressive. If such an idea comes to an actor during a performance because it suddenly occurs to him that he will accomplish more this way with the man with whom he is angry, it means that it has come intuitively, subconsciously, and at a moment of inspiration. He must not, however, repeat it during his next performance without first analyzing and understanding what made him behave in such an unexpected manner. Once he finds the reason, he may use it as a stimulus to this behavior every time he performs the same role.

If an actor receives a suggestion for an adaptation from his director, he must make it his own, not simply accept it. If an actor observes an interesting adaptation in life and thinks it characteristic of his role, he can bring it to the stage, but only after he has made it his own.

When an actor's faculties are functioning on the stage, the creative process takes place and his emotions flow spontaneously; brilliant ideas for adaptations will often come intuitively, subconsciously.

Adaptation is the final element of the actor's inner technique. Each of the elements is a stimulus to the emotions. Each, when carried out fully and with common sense, is capable of awakening the true emotions and of bringing an actor into an inner state in which he will create intuitively, subconsciously. Such a creative state makes inspiration possible.

Each element of the Method affects each actor differently. After studying all of them, an actor will realize which is the most efficient in making his senses function and in thus awakening his emotions. When he uses that one fully, energetically, all the other elements will be involved automatically.

**EXERCISES**

1. You want a favor of the person you meet for lunch. Try to achieve your purpose using means which would be most effective in the case.

2. Your children will return home from school any minute. You do not want them to notice the effect of tragic news on you.

3. You meet a man you were trying to avoid because you owe him an explanation. What would you do?

# 10 TEMPO-RHYTHM

Though Stanislavski did not include *tempo-rhythm* in his first book about the inner technique, it is a powerful stimulus to an actor's emotions. While elements of the Method's inner technique are indirect stimuli to emotions (by making an actor's faculties function), the approach through tempo-rhythm is direct, almost mechanical.

During every minute of life there are tempo (speed) and rhythm (beat) within us as well as outside us. Every movement, every fact or event is taking place in a corresponding tempo-rhythm. We go to our work and come home in different tempo-rhythms; there are different tempo-rhythms inside us when we listen to music and when we listen to a fire siren. We also look at a beautiful landscape and at a traffic accident in different inner tempo-rhythms.

To find an appropriate tempo-rhythm, actors should beat out in an entirely external, rhythmical way (like an orchestra conductor) what they are experiencing inwardly.

When an actor seeks a justified tempo-rhythm for what he is doing, he is directly approaching his emotions which will respond. There is an individual right rhythm in every person. An actor must find it for the character he portrays. It will help him feel correct in his role, and it is as important to him to find it as it is for a director to find the right rhythm for a whole performance.

**EXERCISES**

1. You are having your breakfast. You are late for your work. Find the correct tempo-rhythm.

2. Write different letters. Find the correct inner rhythms.

3. Move with music. Learn to live inwardly with different tempos of music.

# 11 MOTIVE FORCES OF PSYCHOLOGICAL LIFE

The mind, the will, and the emotions are the three forces responsible for our psychological life, and an actor depends on them when he creates a live human being on the stage.

His mind will help an actor to use intelligently the elements of technique which in turn will stir his inner life and his emotions. An actor's mind helps him to have judgment about a play, about his lines, about everything he says or does in his part.

Strong will power is of paramount importance to an actor. It is an actor's will that helps him to concentrate on various objects, that helps him to use his imagination, or to carry out his objectives. It is his will that makes him do what he has to do when he must do it.

Emotions must be evoked if the character an actor creates is to be alive.

When an actor has control over his emotions, will, and mind, he can create and live the life analogous to that of the character he portrays.

# 12 THE UNBROKEN LINE OF A ROLE

To create the complete life of a character in a play, an actor must first of all thoroughly read the play several times, analyze it, and understand the *main idea* of the author. Only after understanding the main idea will the actors and the director begin to feel and to see the characters of the future performance. The main idea is the theme, the spine, and the pulse of the play, in which the character created by an actor is a single element. That is why an actor must know the mission of his character in the chain of events of the play and his responsibility in making the main idea alive. In the theme of his role, which he must clearly see, every detail, every gesture, every thought must be imbued with the light of the basic main idea.

As mentioned in the chapter on imagination, a playwright rarely describes the past or the future, and even omits many details in the present life of his characters. With the help of his imagination, an actor must see in his mind a logical, continuous, unbroken chain of events in the life of his character. All the experiences which through life have influenced the character will help the actor to build his role with justification.

A character is born of the fusion of many elements, among them the influence of the author and the director, contact with other performers, and all the hints in the play about this character.

A role must be connected with everything around it. An actor must establish relationship with other characters. He must know how he feels about everyone and everything that takes place in the play. He must know the environment he is to reflect with his portrayal. He must study the behavior of his character. Whatever an actor does in his role, his clothes, his speech, and his movements must be characteristic of the person he portrays.

Every activity in a role must be justified by the text. The quality of an activity varies with different characters. The search for the right activity is the road to creation of a character or, as Stanislavski calls it, to "reincarnation."

Such reincarnation he considers the height and the crown of an actor's art. If an actor plays only himself and does not create the character, he impoverishes the art of the theater. Creating the character and merging with it is the essence of the theater and is obligatory for actors.

There is nothing mystical, there is no mysterious transformation in Stanislavski's "reincarnation." He follows the same road that writers do in the lives of their characters. The actor controls all his actions on the stage. He is always the master of his character. Though intuition plays an important part in it, the building of a character cannot be intuitive. Stanislavski rejects unconscious creativeness. The building of a character is a conscious process, and an actor will achieve it when he achieves a natural, spontaneous, truthful behavior of the character; when his actions are interwoven with words and thoughts; when he has searched and mastered the traits necessary for the life of the character.

Every action must be carefully selected because it must help to discover the character. An action cannot be accidental or superfluous. The choice of actions must be guided by the main idea (the "super-objective") of the play.

"While portraying an evil person, look for goodness in him," said Stanislavski. Trying to project only evil would make the performance heavy and monotonous. Finding some virtues in an abominable character would make the portrayal truthful and more vivid; the performance would be lighter and more interesting. The really important quality in an actor is his ability to see, to observe, to study life with his eyes, his ears, his heart, and his mind. He must know how to find the necessary—for him typical —material and how to use on the stage what he sees in life. "Genius," said Stanislavski, "is the actor who sees life and is able to reincarnate it on the stage."

In the process of building a character an actor must collect all the possible details and characteristic traits. Sometimes he can find these in the reserve of his memories. Later he should discard the superfluous, because an actor must be concrete. Only what is strictly necessary lives and plays on the stage. Among his accumulated details, an actor should use only those which become necessary, almost obligatory, because they help to individualize a particular personality. Each moment of the role must be expressed by the means that help artistic portrayal: a characteristic external detail can emphasize the thought and sometimes be more expressive than a psychological monologue.

Breaking up his role into units with different objectives will give an actor perspective in his role and help him to know which moments to color or to shade in the best interests of the play. Such breaking up of the role will be helpful in assimilating it better and also in memorizing it.

In order that his character may live a continuous life on the stage, an actor must have *inner monologues* when the other characters speak, for he must react inwardly to everything that takes place on the stage. There are silences or pauses on the stage. These, too, an actor must fill with active thoughts to make life on the stage continuous.

As already explained in the chapter on imagination, the lines of the author are meaningless until an actor analyzes them and gives them the sense that the author intended. It is the meaning, the thoughts, and the inner actions (objectives) which are important, not simply the words. If an actor's imagination is rich and he finds an interesting, logical "subtext," not only will he convey what the author means but he will avoid being monotonous. If an actor honestly and energetically strives to fulfill his objective in each unit, the audience will understand what he wants to say. The inner action brings out the active word. The word that expresses a thought is the most powerful means of projecting concrete traits of a character and of affecting spectators. If the audience does not understand what an actor is saying, the fault lies not alone in defective diction.

In his work on a role an actor should create additional physical or psychological obstacles to overcome (always, of course, entirely justified by the text of the role). For instance, if he has a secret to tell to another person and he thinks that people may hear him, or that somebody may come in and he will not have time to tell it, such imaginary but logical obstacles will force him to fulfill his inner objectives more vividly.

Before speaking his lines an actor must "see" first what he wants to say. He must have an inner vision. This he has to prepare *at home* or, at worst, in rehearsal. But during the performance the visions must come together with the words. This will become habit. As said in the chapter on imagination, an actor's word becomes his own when he has his own concrete vision of the event and the people.

In preparing his role, an actor should play improvisations on various possible situations in which the character might find himself but which are not in the play. Lines not given by the author, but which the character *might* say, should be spoken.

An actor must try to understand the typical traits of the character which he himself does not possess; he must master them, try to behave as if he were the character.

While creating a character an actor must forget all the roles he has ever created previously and each time build a completely new one, the one conceived by the author. A character, though already conceived by the author of the play, must express the actor's individual ideas, his individual moods, his emotions, his intuition—analogous, of course, to those of the character he creates. Only when the actor's personality fuses with the character will the actor reign in his role.

There is a danger in an actor's trying to set the definite form of his role too early. He must bear in mind that at no time has he reached the limit. Art is search, not final form, said Eugene Vakhtangov. If what an actor finds is good, it will be easy to find something better. Even after the opening of the play, the role should grow.

Before a performance, an actor should arrive at the theater sufficiently ahead of his entrance. Besides putting on his costume and his make-up, he needs also to warm up through the *inner technique*. He must make sure that his emotions respond to the stimulus. He should go over the important points of his role, being sure to remember the main idea of the author and that of his role and all his objectives. Looking at the stage and orienting himself will put him into a right relationship to the objects on the stage; seeing why they are there will make him feel comfortable. In his mind an actor should go through what might have happened to him as the character in the play before he appears. He must know the whole day's activity of his character, and if he follows logic his imagination will tell him what he did just before his entrance on the stage. The actor must start playing a minute or two before he goes on. He should come gradually and logically to the moment of his entrance.

# 13 THE ACTOR'S INNER STATE

We already know that when an actor comes on the stage his inner state is very different from a normal inner state in life. Often an actor is frightened, because everything he does or says is being watched by a multitude of people. Faculties which function naturally in life are often paralyzed on the stage. Without the normal functioning of his ability to see, hear, think, to wish, and to move naturally, there is no normal inner state and the actor does not behave as a living human being. To be able to create a truthful character, an actor must revive all his faculties, which means that he must be in a normal functioning state on the stage.

The *inner psychological technique* was developed by

Stanislavski for this purpose. Any element of it when carried out honestly and fully will involve all others and will lead to normal functioning of the faculties. When an actor is in a functioning inner state, which is the creative state, his emotions flow spontaneously and he gets the response of the audience.

With the aid of the inner technique an actor can check his inner state before a performance. This will also help him to be in the atmosphere of the play and of his role and to keep his attention away from the audience.

Without developing details an actor should, before a performance, go over the main points of his role and be sure that his units and objectives are absolutely clear to him. If the role is mature, this takes very little time.

While living the life of his character on the stage the actor must constantly check his inner state, because it is not stable. An experienced actor will do it automatically, and will instantly note the element which, by not functioning properly, is interfering with his creative state. He will immediately correct it. The famous actor Tommaso Salvini said that the very quintessence of the art of the theater was in the double life of the actor on the stage, his balance between real life and performance. He said an actor lives, cries, laughs on the stage, but never stops watching his tears and his laughter.

# 14 THE SUPER-OBJECTIVE AND THE THROUGH-LINE OF ACTION

The theater brings a written play onto the stage; the actors and the director are responsible for the transmission to the public of the author's *main idea*, his theme and reason for having written the play. To carry across the main idea, or the *super-objective*, as Stanislavski calls it, is the final goal of every performance. The super-objective must always be clear in the mind of an actor, from the beginning and throughout the play to its very end, and he must remember his responsibility to make it alive with everything he does in his role. Every detail, every thought, every objective must be closely related to the super-objective in order to help carry it across. If an actor does not know his mission in this respect, his role and the whole play will suffer.

To remember easily the super-objective an actor should give it a name which should be an active verb, because that will give impetus to the process of achieving it. A right and expressive name for the super-objective is of great significance—the interpretation of the play depends on it.

Just as in every unit of a role (see Chapter V) there is an obstacle to overcome in carrying out an objective, so in every play there is a counteraction to the super-objective. An actor must know precisely what it is, because his energetic attempt to overcome it will make the performance vivid.

In order that an actor's performance may have logical order and perspective, he should trace a line which will run through his role. Stanislavski calls this the *through-line of action.* It is all the actor's actions interwoven logically, following the same road, having the same purpose of expressing dynamically the *main idea* (the super-objective) of the dramatist.

This line in the actor's mind, its essential meaning close to the *role's* main idea, will keep all the elements of his role in logical order and will help him to follow the right road toward projecting the super-objective. An actor must constantly check his through-line of action to make sure that everything he is doing has order, logic, the right activity, color, contrast, etc., and to make sure that all these elements contribute to the projection of the super-objective.

The search for the super-objective, for the through-line of action, and for the theme of a role is called by Stanislavski *reconnaissance of the mind*.

Just as he has a super-objective and a through-line of action in a role, the actor must have them in every exercise or improvisation.

# 15 THE SUBCONSCIOUS IN THE INNER CREATIVE STATE

The Method's essential purpose is to bring an actor into an inner creative state when he is on the stage. As we know, every element of the Method's *inner technique* can affect each actor differently. An actor must find out which of the elements will be the most effective clue to the normal functioning of *his* human faculties. He must use the one that is the most effective for him fully, energetically. All other elements of the inner technique will then become automatically involved in his work and he will reach the inner creative state, when his emotions will flow spontaneously.

When, with the aid of the Method's inner technique, an actor functions as a live human being, he feels comfortable. His subconscious then has been reached through entirely conscious means and he creates naturally, subconsciously, intuitively. In such a creative inner state, which is the *I am* state, when an actor lives and merges with his character he will give an inspired performance.

## 16 THE ACTOR'S PHYSICAL APPARATUS

With his means of expression, which are his face, his voice, his movements, and his emotions, an actor must keep the attention of the spectators and be able to carry them away. He must impress and stir them in any kind of play. To keep the attention of a great number of people in the audience is difficult, and an actor must make sure that while creating a character not a single nuance is lost, not any physical or psychological means which would help to express his inner experience. A slight movement of the head, of the fingers, a change in the direction of a look, will tell about the inner life of the character and will project his thoughts.

Unfortunately, few know or remember that Stanislavski said that the art of the theater was based on the union of the deep substance of the inner life and a beautiful, light, expressive form of it. The expressiveness of the whole performance depends upon this union; there cannot be real *art* without it.

The quality of an actor's performance depends not only upon the creation of the inner life of a role, but also upon the physical embodiment of it. Stanislavski said that imperfection in the external expression of a role can disfigure a profound conception of the playwright.

In order to embody the subtle inner life of a character, an actor must have at his command responsive and sensitive physical means. The actor's body and voice must be cultivated and trained to be able to express externally, instantly and precisely, the delicate inner experiences of the creative process. The inner and the physical apparatus of an actor must be trained simultaneously.

Stanislavski believed in training the body to improve posture and to make movements supple, graceful, and finished. An actor must, however, bear in mind that there is no place in the living theater for mannerisms or mechanical gestures. An actor should not use a gesture because it is graceful or plastic. A gesture must reflect an inner experience. It will then become a purposeful, logical, and truthful movement.

Daily practice in dance, ballet-bar work, fencing, rhythm, plastic movement, and acrobatics are necessary to have an adequate physical apparatus.

An actor must also have systematic lessons in voice and diction. His voice must be trained like that of a singer and be placed in the "masque," the front of the face where there are resonators. Speech on the stage is as important an art as singing is for a singer. When an actor has a well-developed respiration, a good clear diction, and a trained voice, he will not have to force it, but instead will be able to speak naturally and softly, and even his whisper will be heard everywhere in the theater.

# 17 PERSPECTIVE

Perspective in a part is the harmonious relationship and distribution of everything an actor does in his role—his actions, thoughts, movements, in connection with the whole play. (An actor must clearly divide the perspective in the life of his character from that which he as an actor has when building his character.) When an actor has perspective, he has brought the important objectives into relief and into the foreground, and has pushed onto a secondary plane others less important. He has added variety, contrast, coloring, and shading to his role's various moments. He distributes all the elements of his role and his expressive and effective means in a harmonious way in the interest of the play, and his role grows logically.

# BIBLIOGRAPHY

# BIBLIOGRAPHY

*Complete Works of Stanislavski.* Six volumes. Moscow: Iskusstvo, 1954–1959.

*My Life in Art,* by K. S. Stanislavski. Moscow, 1925, Academy Moscow, 1928.

*Stanislavski's Theatrical Legacy,* edited by E. Grabar, S. Durylin and P. Markov. Moscow: Academy of Science of the USSR, 1955.

*The Directorial Lessons of K. S. Stanislavski,* by N. M. Gorchakov. Moscow: Iskusstvo, 1950.

*K. S. Stanislavski on the Director's Work with An Actor,* by N. M. Gorchakov, Moscow, 1958.

*The Moscow Art Theater,* edited by N. Chushkin. Moscow: Iskusstvo, 1955.

*Actors Discuss Vakhtangov,* compiled by H. Khersonski. Moscow-Leningrad, 1940.

*The Directorial Lessons of Vakhtangov,* by N. M. Gorchakov. Moscow: Iskusstvo, 1957.

*Ivan Moskvin on the Stage of the Moscow Art Theater,* by V. Y. Vilenkin. Moscow: Museum of the Moscow Art Theater. 1946.

*Vassily Ivanovich Kachalov,* compiled and edited by V. Y. Vilenkin. Moscow: Iskusstvo, 1954.

*Glikeria Fedotova,* by Georg Goyan. Moscow: Iskusstvo, 1940.

## Bibliography

*Maria Nikolaevna Ermolova,* by S. N. Durylin. Moscow: Academy of Science, 1953.

*Museum of the Moscow Art Theater.* Moscow: The Moscow Worker, 1958.

The following works by Stanislavski have been translated into English:

*My Life in Art,* translated by J. J. Robbins. Boston: Little, Brown, 1924.

*An Actor Prepares,* translated by Elizabeth R. Hapgood. New York: Theatre Arts, 1936.

*Building a Character,* translated by Elizabeth R. Hapgood. New York: Theatre Arts, 1949.

*Stanislavski's Legacy,* edited and translated by Elizabeth R. Hapgood. New York: Theatre Arts, 1958.